Poems of Merthyr

*W*ithin
the
*P*ast

Ashley O'Keefe

Independently Published

Copyright © 2022
Ashley O'Keefe

ISBN: 9798364074614

Contents

FOREWORD

When I was asked to write this foreword I was chuffed to bits. As many of you know Ashley and I have a number of joint books published (the 'Rhianno & Asley' poetry collections). We have different approaches to our writing, but we click creatively, and this is why I feel qualified to write this foreword - I'm one of the people who knows his poetry best.

I'm also in the unique position to roll my eyes when he tells me he has writer's block... because he hasn't written for a whole day!

In this beautiful book, 'Within the Past: Poems of Merthyr' Ashley takes us on a nostalgic journey through the places he has known and loved. Through his eyes, or rather, words, and set against a stunning valleys backdrop, we experience the heart, history and culture of Merthyr Tydfil and surrounding areas.

Family, memories and reflection... Colourful local characters fondly recalled. From the legacy of this thriving industry based on iron, and later coal, to Nature's reclamation of those abandoned, pit-scarred hills, this is Merthyr in all of its light and shade.

Writing comes so naturally to Ashley, and people really connect with his words and the gorgeous visual imagery in his poems. He writes the way that he feels - never pretentious nor a slave to (often restrictive) 'forms' of poetry. Ashley's words come to him spontaneously, and a really beautiful part of his talent is how he can write so concisely yet with such depth of meaning. I am forever in awe of his intrinsic sense of rhythm and emotion - Ashley is always true to himself!

I defy anyone not to be charmed by this exceptional poetry book. A tribute from a superbly talented writer to the place he was born, raised and still lives to this day.

I'm as proud as punch to count myself not only as his writing partner and co-author but also as his friend. I only wish I was able to express as Ashley can in so few words... but that skill evades me, and for this I apologise to you dear reader.

Enjoy this beautiful poetry collection!

Rhiannon Owens

INTRODUCTION

This is the book I've been wanting to complete for some time.

Having written a number of poems about Merthyr and its alluring countryside and rich history, I've always wanted to put them together in one volume, and in this book, I have finally achieved it.

I was born in Trefechan in the sixties, moving to Cefn Coed in the early seventies where I still live today. My wife, Helen and I have raised two beautiful daughters here.

I have enjoyed the captivating scenery and history surrounding our famous town all my life and hope to bring this across within these pages.

This book has truly been a local passion project, a labour of love...

I really hope you enjoy it.

If there's to be a collection of poems about Merthyr Tydfil and its past, then why not start with how the town got its name.

'Martyr' Tydfil

One of many daughters
To a 5th century king,
To Brychan of Brycheiniog
Tydfil's religious life would begin,

From within a monastic community
A small band of people she would lead,
With compassion and skilful healing
Nursing the sick, of man or animal breed,

Building them a small church
Made from wattle and daub,
Within the settlement's enclosure
To keep from turning to Staub…

A raiding party attacked
Her people ran, they fought,
Murdered, butchered, massacred
For spoils they came; they sought,

Tydfil, they came to find
Before going on their way,
Kneeling in her church
Cut down while she prayed,

A burial within her church
A cross to mark the place,
A site for future pilgrimage
A stone church to replace.

Ashley O'Keefe

Tydfil
Illustration by Dewi Bowen
Courtesy of Liz Bowen

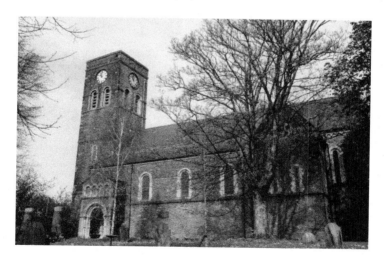

St. Tydfil's Old Parish Church
Courtesy of Molly O'Keefe taken April 2022

Standing at the lower end of Merthyr Tydfil High Street, St Tydfil's Old Parish Church was built to keep sacred the spot where Tydfil was martyred because of her Christian beliefs.

IRONWORKS TO GALLOWS:

YNYSFACH IRONWORKS
Illustration by Dewi Bowen
Courtesy of Liz Bowen

A Poetic Synopsis covering the Merthyr Uprising of 1831.

Written by Ashley O'Keefe and narrated by Alan Johnson

Dedicated to Dewi Bowen

YouTube Link: -
https://www.youtube.com/watch?v=yi-EUCgovBg&t=41s

From a Hoot to a Whistle

Hues of mango, peach and pink
Above the skyline to the east,
Slowly bleeding into blue
At Summer's dawning feast,

Suddenly, the sun breaks through
A fire along the horizon's edge,
Slowly revealing glowing gold
Pouring warmth over its ledge,

Surrounded by rocky hills and woods
Mountain streams and rivers flow,
The sound of birdsong fills the air
A picture of rural life begins to grow,

Farmhouses scatter around a village amongst fields
A church and a corn mill stand,
So picturesque, so unspoiled
Life in a tranquil land,

Then with a hoot, summer's evening sets
To the west, the day turns to dusk,
Light ebbs with the warmth of the day
Soil parched like a fibrous husk,

The silence of twilight in the midnight blue
The sky darkens, tranquillity transforms,
The hoot from the owl morphs into a steam whistle
As darkness descends and swarms,

Deep into darkness, now a smoky landscape
Where chimney stacks billow and blast furnaces roar,
Tartarean, dismal, unwelcoming

A new home for the lonely and poor,

An irruption of industry with its man-made volcanoes
Waiting patiently to erupt,
A constant reminder to the inhabitants
This place, its purpose; their hands cupped,

An infernal scene of wild figures
Workmen broiling in sweat and dirt,
Amid the furnaces and rolling mills
The Masters wanting them to spurt,

Within this gloomy transformation
Around the ironworks, slum houses quickly grow,
Crammed together, a barracks for industry
Within the town, open sewers flow,

People flock in hope for a better life
To this 'Little Hell' they all come,
Overcrowded, living in squalor
Disease and poverty in a dismal slum.

Ashley O'Keefe

Watercolour by local artist Ken Morgan

Vision of Hell

From the top of the mountain
Gazing down in darkness at the lurid light,
In the distance, the ironworks
At night it comes to life,

The POUNDING of huge hammers
CLANKING of the chain,
The WHIZ of wheels, BLAST of bellows
An incessant din of pain,

The vivid GLOW and ROARING
Hungry furnaces SPEWING SMOKE and FLAME,
Waiting to be fed
A vision of HELL to tame.

Ashley O'Keefe

Dowlais Ironworks
Illustration by Dewi Bowen
Courtesy of Liz Bowen

The Masters Grin

Smoke from the ironworks darkens the sky
Smuts of filth give the town its dingy air,
Young sooty children barefoot and in rags
Play in the street while some of them stare,

Protesters VOICES
With banners, they CHANT
"REFORM" and "END TO POVERTY"

The Masters, they MOCK
They don't understand
Inequality.

Passing the Castle Inn, the downtrodden march
While upstairs, the masters grin,
Around the food table, they laugh and they joke
Fill their bellies then start to sing,

Protesters VOICES
With banners, they CHANT
"REFORM" and "END TO POVERTY"

The Masters, they MOCK
They don't understand
Inequality.

Finishing a lavish meal, the Masters rise
Take their wine glass to the window with song,
They look down on the people, they sip their wine
Oblivious to the fact something's wrong,

Protesters VOICES
With banners, they CHANT

"REFORM" and "END TO POVERTY"

The Masters, they MOCK
They don't understand
Inequality.

Ashley O'Keefe

**Merthyr Tydfil High Street 1847 or later showing
The Castle Inn on the right, below Abbotts Barber Shop**
Courtesy of Cyfarthfa Castle Museum and Art Gallery

© *Rob Amos 2018*

6

Clutching Her Bread

Two bailiffs knock
With an ear-splitting BANG!
The door frame splinters
As if hit by a ram,

The door swings open
With an almighty BOOM!
Hanging by its hinge
It sways in the room,

A sick, old woman
Lies in her bed,
The head bailiff enters
And SHOUTS "Pay or be bled..."

... the bailiffs emerge
From the house with a bed,
The old woman lies floored
STARTLED, clutching her bread,

The heavy burden of life
Written deep in her FACE,
Her weary, listless EYES
Welling up, TEARS trace.

Ashley O'Keefe

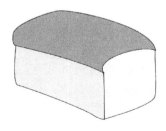

Her Sorrowful Sound

In a gloomy graveyard
The smoke of industry hangs in the air,
A man and a woman
The man says a prayer,

A Mother's voice
Her sorrowful sound,
Humming a nursery rhyme
As the coffin's lowered into the ground,

Standing with the Minister
Like death; withering and weary,
It won't be too long
Before she joins her little dearie,

Not a tear in her eye
It's the final blow,
In a state of shock
She's no more left to show.

Ashley O'Keefe

Rising

Working boots pace
Along the ground,
Purposeful strides
To a rising sound,

A blood-soaked flag
Hangs from a pole,
Carried by a man
Who digs out the coal,

In a town's gloomy atmosphere
Though the black smoke has cleared,
The furnaces now hushed
It's time the shopkeepers feared,

Chanting with banners
Destroying Coffin's Court,
Marching around the town
Seeking reform and support,

Raiding and seizing
Houses for their goods,
Restoring to their owners
Yet some taken by the hoods,

The Magistrate Bruce
Can't make them see sense,
Tempers have been frayed
The whole matter, so tense,

There's nothing more for it
But to send for assistance,
From the military at Brecon

They must travel some distance.

Ashley O'Keefe

Illustration by Dewi Bowen
Courtesy of Liz Bowen

Twenty Miles to Merthyr

In night's darkness
A torch flame lights up the sign,
'Twenty Miles to Merthyr'
Those Brecon soldiers march in line,

Along that dusty road
Under pale moonlight,
Below a glint of stars
Toward the Iron Town this night…

The morning sun, she rises
Those soldiers marching on,
Sweating and weary, no longer cheery
Too tired to sing their song,

In the heat so oppressive
Within that sultry air,
The thunder looming closer
Through the village people stare,

Women and children line the street
They laugh, they mock, they jeer,
Taunting those men in kilts
The men that they should fear,

Marching from the village
Followed by moans and groans,
Women armed with broomsticks
Their children carry stones,

From the road up ahead
Comes a blood-chilling sound,
Low snarling voices

As those feet parade the ground,

Louder and louder the mutterings
Grow into the roar of a mob,
So many soldiers wishing
They had some other job,

The vanguard of the crowd
Fills the road up ahead,
With their home-made banner
A flag, coloured red,

A crowd ready for trouble
Hundreds carry clubs and picks,
Shaking their weapons in the air
Firing insults just for kicks,

An Officer in a stentorian voice
Bellows for the crowd to fall back,
"We are under orders of the King"
Please God, don't let them attack,

As the column approach, the crowd slowly part
Opening like the Red Sea,
Keeping to both sides of the road
Not to be driven into town prematurely,

With the crowd looming all around
They begin to hiss and shout,
At those exhausted hungry soldiers
Whose sweat burning eyes dart about,

In Welsh, the cries and insults
Continue through the narrow street,
Arriving at the Castle Inn

The Ironmasters come out to greet.

Ashley O'Keefe

Illustration by Dewi Bowen
Courtesy of Liz Bowen

Merthyr's Rising

The riot act; read
The delegation; out,
"We'll do all we can"
The Ironmasters shout,
For 'bread and cheese'
For 'blood or bread',
Refusing to disperse
Merthyr's rising instead,
Angry stares
Frightened glares,
Soldiers rushing
Up the stairs,
From an upper window
Guest and Crawshay plead,
Below, standing on a chair
The Sheriff demands they leave,
At the first-floor windows
As rehearsed many times before,
Soldiers ready their muskets
This is now their war,
On the pavement below
The crowd and soldiers lock,
Surging forward from the rear
Bayonets and clubs shake and shock,
Pushing and shoving
Tumult ringing all about,
Clubbing and beating
Those bayonets thrusting out,
In furious desperation
Muskets ripped from hand,
Bludgeoned, stabbed, and wrestled
Like gladiators to the sand,
Then, a volley of musket fire

Billowing; a white cloud,
Obscuring the people's panic
As they fall wrapped in their shroud,
Bloodied, battered, wounded
One for all, and all for bread,
Fingers twitch, a lifeless hand
Many lie amongst their dead...
... As the musket smoke clears
There's a soldier who's been stabbed,
And for the sake of pride
A barber's vengeance grabbed.

Ashley O'Keefe

Illustration by Dewi Bowen
Courtesy of Liz Bowen

Illustration by Dewi Bowen
Courtesy of Liz Bowen

Illustration by Dewi Bowen
Courtesy of Liz Bowen

The Song of a Martyr

Led by the hangman
There's reluctance in the air,
A restless sky grumbles
To the people's empty glare,

The silence disrupted
By a thunderous roar,
The rain pours down
Where droplets scattered before,

Murmurs from the gathering
Motionless and wet,
The rain soaks their skin
Like fish in the net,

And as the sky blackens
On the sombre scene,
A shock of brilliant white
Blinding and unforeseen.

He walks to the gallows
Wrists strapped behind,
Scanning the crowd
For his bride, he must find,

He climbs up the steps
Onto the platform,
Placed beneath the rope
For the forthcoming storm,

As the hood comes down
Over his eyes,
With his wife he shares glances

They both share sad smiles,

Under his breath
He says a little prayer,
'O Lord what an injustice'
As the noose comes to bear,

From within the blackness
His heavy breathing quickens,
With the clunk of the lever
His stomach sickens,

The gasp of the crowd
The sudden rush,
The falling, the struggle
The feeling, the crush,

The rope now taut
Creaks and swings,
To the song of a martyr
It bitterly sings.

Ashley O'Keefe

Illustration by Dewi Bowen
Courtesy of Liz Bowen

The Angels Give Their Wings

Heads bow amongst cries
Suddenly, a SCREAM!
The death shadow sways
A young body to redeem,

An hour passed
His body cut down,
Day turns to night
In a sorrowful town…

… A new day dawns
With the sun's breaking light,
Its rays of gold
Can't unspoil the blight,

Looking down from the heavens
At the river of people,
Along country roads
Heading for a steeple,

A funeral procession
Shoulder to shoulder,
Following his Gambo
As a sad day grows colder,

A farm cart holds a coffin
In which he lay,
This is the price
For a scapegoat to pay,

Now at his graveside
A young boy sadly sings,
'God bless Dic Penderyn'

As the angels give their wings.

Ashley O'Keefe

St Mary's Church c1850, Aberavon
Illustration by Dewi Bowen
Courtesy of Liz Bowen

Richard Lewis (Dic Penderyn) was buried in St Mary's Churchyard where a memorial was placed in 1966. There is a plaque to Dic Penderyn at Cardiff Market, near to the gallows site.

LIFE IN THE 1800s:

YNYSGAU
Illustration by Dewi Bowen
Courtesy of Liz Bowen

Hear Her Still

Wicker basket swinging
Scuffed leather boots skip,
Shabby dress with a pinafore
In its thick material, a rip,

Humming a sweet tune
As she skips along,
Her head, her heart
So full of song,

To the market on an errand
She must run,
Her young soul so happy
Full of life and fun...

... Wicker basket broken
Strewn upon the ground,
With a scuffed leather boot
Was all that they found...

... On those cold lonely nights
You can hear her still,
Humming and skipping
Through Winter's chill.

Ashley O'Keefe
(Inspired by Lynette Rees's book 'The Workhouse Waif')

23

Time to Gloat

The hustle, the bustle
The market life,
Its colours, its smells
Sounds of chopping, the knife,

A young boy loiters
Near a fruit and veg stall,
Gangly, skinny
His clothes make him look small,

They're tattered, they're old
They've seen better days,
His flat cap; too big
Covers his eyes and his gaze,

Looking suspicious
Up to no good,
He's starving, he's hungry
He wants to be good,

One shiny red apple
Slips inside his coat,
No more is he seen
He's moved on, time to gloat,

The hustle, the bustle
The market life,
The chopping has ceased
In search of the knife.

Ashley O'Keefe
(Inspired by Lynette Rees's book 'The Workhouse Waif')

Stale Beer

A door hauled open
Draws in the cold,
A bellowing voice
In anger will scold,

Awoken, shaken
Fumes of stale beer,
Freezing in terror
Trembling with fear,

Dragged from the hearth
Yanked by the collar,
A young stomach rolling
And churning in horror,

A neck tightly grasped
Like a fish in the net,
Bloodshot bulging eyes
A mouth's spittle; corners wet,

Unable to breathe
Gagging for breath,
To pass out or to vomit
Or to meet one's own death.

Ashley O'Keefe
(Inspired by Lynette Rees's book 'The Workhouse Waif')

Secret Dreams

Lying in darkness
All lights are out,
Gazing at stars
There's love to think about,

This time yesterday
He didn't exist,
Now all she can think of...
Her mind will persist,

Floating along moonbeams
Flying amongst stars,
Humming her tune
To be lost without scars,

Falling so gently
So softly to sleep,
A smile in her eyes
Secret dreams she will keep.

Ashley O'Keefe
(Inspired by Lynette Rees's book 'The Workhouse Waif')

Emotions Swim

Lying still
Covered in grey,
Tired eyes; closed
Skin sallow and pale,

Peppered hair
Clings to face,
Long, unkempt
Life lost, no trace,

Young searching hands
Reaching out,
Icy cold
Beyond all doubt,

Realisation
Sweeping in,
A feeling of dread
Seeping under young skin,

Old, stone cold
Rigid limb,
Stiff as boards
Young emotions swim.

Ashley O'Keefe
(Inspired by Lynette Rees's book 'The Workhouse Waif')

To the Workhouse

A day of grey
Shrouded in mist,
Softly rain falls
Heaven sends out its kiss,

Children now whimper
Toddlers hanging on,
They don't understand
The old death song,

A last glimpse of the coffin
In silence, a tear,
Now orphaned, alone
To the workhouse, in fear.

Ashley O'Keefe
(Inspired by Lynette Rees's book 'The Workhouse Waif')

Away We Must Run

Dust coated windows; broken
Walls blackened with mold,
A house looking empty
Doesn't keep out the cold,

A ramshackle door; wooden
Peeling with paint,
Slowly swings open
In the doorway, a young gent,

His eyes blinking open
His eyes open wide,
In shock, disbelief
"Is it really you?", he cried,

He looks so much thinner
Darker under the eyes,
So gaunt, so unwell
Two hearts bleed with their cries,

"Of course it is me
I said I would come,
I've come here to find you
Now away we must run".

Ashley O'Keefe
(Inspired by Lynette Rees's book 'The Workhouse Waif')

Humiliation

A message of humiliation
Hanging from her neck,
Chalk written on a slate,
Just to keep them all in check,

"The idle suffer hunger"
It reads across her chest,
She hears someone snigger
Her only crime... a rest,

Now upon a wooden podium
She's made to stand amongst the stares,
Lightheaded, dizzy, feeling faint
And nobody even cares,

The new Master and his Matron
Enforce strict Workhouse rule,
No more dilly-dallying
You'll work hard for your gruel!

Special privileges granted to the rats
Who'll sell their souls for extra shares,
To make some poor young innocent
Stand up and face the glares.

Ashley O'Keefe
(Inspired by Lynette Rees's book 'The Workhouse Waif')

The Shame

From the Master's room
She runs in floods of tears,
Shaking, devastated
Adjusts her clothes, avoids the leers,

Back to her dorm
To hide away in her bed,
The shame, the scratches, the bruises
Strangulated words inside her head,

Weeping turns to sobbing
What that filthy waster made her do,
She knows it won't be the last
He'll now constantly pursue.

Ashley O'Keefe
(Inspired by Lynette Rees's book 'The Workhouse Waif')

Cakes

Packing up
At the end of the day,
Not much left on the stall
And since it goes stale anyway,

She gave what was left
To the boy teaching his dog tricks,
With no meat on his bones
And his legs like sticks,

She watched as he ate
Enjoying the cakes,
He shared with his dog
Both as thin as rakes,

He had nothing in life
But he shared what he had,
He was kindness itself
And it made her so glad,

He'd been badly treated
But he still cared,
His bumps and bruises
Never showed he was scared...

They laughed, they blushed
Till they were beetroot red,
Her heartbeat quickened
Warm glowing thoughts in her head,

She ran to him
And planted a kiss,
He smiled with surprise

In that moment, "Oh Miss".

Ashley O'Keefe
(Inspired by Lynette Rees's 'The Workhouse Waif')

My Promise to You

In the blink of an eye
Not believing her ears,
"You're leaving for London?"
"I'm afraid so, now no tears,

Don't look so downhearted
I've been waiting for this,
To set foot on that stage
To sing out would be bliss,

I simply must go
No one understands,
What I need in my life
I've so much to give, I've got plans..."

With her eyes filling up
Her young heart reaching out,
A lump in her throat
She just nodded in doubt,

Both hugging so warmly
Tears soaking their sleeves,
Sniffles and smiles
Producing clean handkerchieves,

Drying their eyes
'Cause it just wouldn't do,
"When you go, I will miss you..."
"One day I'll return... that's my promise to you".

Ashley O'Keefe
(Inspired by Lynette Rees's book 'The Workhouse Waif')

Not in Her Bed

"Has anybody seen her?
She's not in her bed,"
"She's been awfully quiet
Not a word has she said,"

Through the Workhouse they searched
Where could she be?
No one had seen her
Since around quarter to three,

The water was still
The water was cold,
Her body was shrivelled
That's what they were told.

Her eyes wide open
Her deathly stare,
An empty gin bottle
Lay beside her, "Right there!".

Ashley O'Keefe
(Inspired by Lynette Rees's book 'The Workhouse Waif')

Missing Piece

Young love blossoms,
Young love blooms,
But turned on its head,
Love is lost, and loss looms...

He's just disappeared
Gone without trace,
Taken away
With a bruise on his face...

Lost on her own
Feeling all alone,
Will he ever come back?
Will he ever come home...?

… Over ten years pass
Then one darkling night,
A knock at her door
A voice by lamplight,

Unfamiliar, well-spoken
She was unafraid,
Slowly opening the door
He stood tall, and she gazed,

"Do you not recognise me?"
He said dressed in his wealth,
So astoundingly handsome
She couldn't catch her breath,

"Do you remember the little boy
With a gleam in his eye?"
Robbed of all breath

She began to tear, then cry,

"Is it really you?" she cried
And fell into his arms,
Lost in his sweet embrace
Overjoyed with his charms,

Her heart now found its missing piece
He was back home to stay,
Looking into each other's eyes
Knowing nothing would get in their way.

Ashley O'Keefe
(Inspired by Lynette Rees's book, 'The Workhouse Waif')

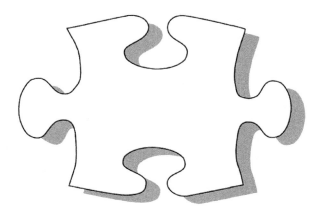

Two Carpet Bags

Entering the house
For the very last time,
Feeling so sad
As her memory clocks chime,

Standing, staring
A voice warning in her head,
'Act quickly, be gone'
Her fear and her dread,

Two carpet bags, she fills
Her heart racing at the thought,
He might come home early
And she might be caught,

Her ears pricked at every sound
That the old house made,
Her belongings now packed
Sitting at the table; afraid,

Penning a letter
The words don't come easily,
Crumpled pieces of paper
Thrown into the fire frequently,

There, finally done
A shard of guilt piercing her heart,
But it's time to escape
Time to make a new start,

One last look around
Say goodbye to the room,
Just as she's leaving

The door bursts open, BOOM!

Staggering, slovenly
Into the affray,
Tears run down her cheeks
Puts her carpet bags away.

Ashley O'Keefe
(Inspired by Lynette Rees's book, 'The Workhouse Waif')

Plentiful and Penniless

He sits at his table
Indulgent, he dines,
She shows her cleavage
In the public house and behind,

He eats a fine meal
Into a napkin, a burp,
She hoists up her garb
Looks away as men slurp,

He thanks the young maid
His eyes smile with a flirt,
She picks up the pennies
Men throw into the dirt,

Plentiful and penniless
Two different lives,
One's life in the gutter
As the other one thrives.

Ashley O'Keefe

Creak of the Cart

CLIP-CLOP
CREAK of the cart
Turning of the wheels,

To pastures new
They say "dreams come true"
So quickly on their heels...

Wheels turned
Families churned
Plodding, marching feet,

Over ground
Winding paths
Riding through the street,

Mothers, fathers
Children too
Migrants from all parts,

Seeking work
And prosperity
In this Iron Town, it starts...

Ashley O'Keefe
(Inspired by a Dewi Bowen illustration)

On Its Way

The CRACK of a whip
Horses NEIGH,

Manes aflame
A coach on its way...

From place to place
A schedule to keep,

Out of a small window
Passengers would peek...

CRACK of the whip
Horses NEIGH,

Manes aflame
The coach on its way...

Ashley O'Keefe
(Inspired by a Dewi Bowen illustration)

Huts of Stone

The district of China
Between the Taff and the Tip,
Mere huts of stone
Unventilated, ill-lit,
A maze of courts
And tortuous lanes,
Unpassable in places
Refuse and filth it contains,
Below ground levels
Where ladders descend,
A place called 'The Cellars'
Where no one's your friend,
Here lives crime and disease
The stench of poverty,
Thieves, prostitutes and vagrants
Degradation, suffering and misery.

Ashley O'Keefe
(Inspired by a Dewi Bowen illustration)

43

Led by the Hand

Beyond the arched entrance
A hive of sin and crime,
Hiding in the darkness
Amongst shadows, filth and grime,

A notorious den
Of thieves and rogues,
Drunkards and prostitutes
Whom an Emperor controls,

The district of China
A dangerous slum,
Many young men entered
With their purses they'd come,

And with a harlot and trickster
Led by the hand,
Now they're lying face down
In the River Taff sand.

Ashley O'Keefe
(Inspired by 'The Ghosts of China' by G I Lewis)

44

Companion piece to 'Led by the Hand':-

The Plan was Simple

He grabbed her from the archway
The constable dragged the harlot back,
Pursued by the Emperor's cronies
He was lucky to avoid attack,
She was quick to give up her accomplices
Once the right pressure was applied,
According to her, "the plan was simple"
"Rob the man... but murder!..."she was horrified,
Each of those responsible
Were arrested and now would sing,
By the time the courts had finished with them
From the gallows they would swing.

Ashley O'Keefe
(Inspired by 'The Ghosts of China' by G I Lewis)

Pontstorehouse Shop, Bethesda Street - 1890s
Courtesy of Alan George's Old Merthyr Tydfil
http://www.alangeorge.co.uk

FULL STEAM AHEAD:

CEFN PONTYCAPEL VIADUCT
Illustration by Dewi Bowen
Courtesy of Liz Bowen

Built in 1866 to carry the Brecon and Merthyr Railway across the Taf Fawr river. The viaduct was curved to avoid land owned by the ironmaster Robert Thompson Crawshay.

First of its Kind

The heat
The steam
The mechanical force,

The pressure
Pushing
Pistons back and forth…

The transformation
Into rotational force,
By connecting rod
And flywheel of course,

Trevithick's steam locomotive
The very first of its kind,
Hauls a train along Merthyr's tramway
Out of an inventor's engineering mind.

Ashley O'Keefe

Trevithick Memorial
Courtesy of Rhiannon Owens taken June 2022

Descendants of Kings (Part 1)

An eerie echo
A whispering breath,
Throughout the town
A gust like death...

...Winter's cold wind blows
Through ragged shawls,
A baby's cry shrills
Another one bawls,

Falls on ironmen's ears
In rough working clothes,
Who jostle with the gentry
In their finery pose,

Fiery Celtic men
Descendants of Kings,
Swearing, spitting
Their moving mass sings...

... Small boys snow fight
Wipe runny nose,
Upon green sleeves
Their cleanliness shows,

Working women
All shapes and sizes,
Nudge perfumed ladies
In resplendent guises,

Heels kick out
Horses shyer,
Misty breath

Around a brazier fire,

Flurries of snow
Float through air,
Upon the street
Winter's freezing glare...

... Shifty eyes flitter
From pocket to purse...

... The imminent plunder
Before the crowds disperse.

Ashley O'Keefe
(Inspired by the book: Iron Horse by Arthur Watkins - Merthyr in the 1800s)

Illustration by Dewi Bowen
Courtesy of Liz Bowen

Merthyr's Eyes (Part 2)

History in the making!
Before our very eyes...

Red-rimmed,
Staring wide,
A rolling sea
Of ten thousand eyes,

EYES!

Saucy, winking,
Bleary, blinking,
Button bright
Baby's eyes thinking,

This strange monstrosity
Menacingly poised,
With piston arms ready
Through history's toils,

EYES!

Wicked, wanton
Shifty, sly,
Eyes stare in wonder
Beneath a Merthyr sky,

This incredible invention
Of a creditable Cornishman,
Such foresight, ingenuity
Such a master plan,

HISS of steam

Friction SCREAM,
TUMULTUOUS crowd
An engineer's DREAM,

Trevithick's coat comes off
Feeding coal to the boiler,
Appetite appeased
For both engine and employer,

SNORTING steam
CHAFING at the bit,
This Iron Horse
With Iron to transmit,

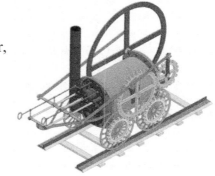

A soot-soiled coat
Whirling above Trevithick's head,
Saluting the crowd
"The Iron Horse has been fed"!

A LEVER pulled
To an avalanche of CHEERS,
As it PULLS away
Merthyr's EYES fill with tears.

Ashley O'Keefe
(Inspired by the book: Iron Horse by Arthur Watkins – Merthyr in the 1800s)

In 1804, Trevithick's steam locomotive pulled ten tons of iron and approximately seventy ironworkers nine miles from the ironworks at Penydarren to the Merthyr – Cardiff Canal, travelling at five miles per hour.

Clickety Clack *(The Brecon Mountain Railway)*

Along the narrow-gauge rails
CLICKETY CLACK,
Over the ballast
Up the track,

HUFFING and PUFFING
The whistle BLOWS,
Climbing northwards
Along the reservoirs it goes,

Pontsticill, Pentwyn
Onwards it goes,
To Torpantau railway station
It arrives... it SLOWS…

Ashley O'Keefe

Watercolour by local artist Ken Morgan

The Seven Arches

In the pre-war era
The high point of the year,
An annual Sunday School outing
Was many people's summer cheer,
From their local station
Catching that Merthyr to Brecon train,
To Pontsarn they would travel
Take refreshment, then entertain,
Beneath those seven arches
The laughter and the fun,
Playing games throughout the day
Until the day was done,
Below that Pontsarn viaduct
Next to the Taf Fechan river,
A place of natural beauty
Above the Blue Pool's water giver.

Ashley O'Keefe

Pontsarn Viaduct
Courtesy of Molly O'Keefe taken April 2022

The Graceful Curve

On the north-western edge of Merthyr
Two rivers meet at their confluence,
Between the Taff Fawr and Taff Fechan
A village lies with and without affluence,

Within the Community of Vaynor
The village of Cefn Coed,
A route built to carry people and wares
Then later to be destroyed,

Fifteen arches in the Cefn Pontycapel Viaduct
Built with a beautiful, graceful curve,
To skirt around Crawshay land
For a Merthyr and Brecon railway to serve.

Ashley O'Keefe

Cefn Pontycapel Viaduct
Courtesy of Molly O'Keefe taken April 2022

Iron-Will

A town forged in iron
And later coal,
Moulded by industry
Workers… the heart and soul,

When the wheels stopped turning
Scarred hillsides were left,
A mighty town sleeping
The people bereft,

(Do you hear in the wind
Echoes of the past?
Hammer on anvil
Memories that last?)

Innovation,
Canals, a tramroad,
Rails straining, creaking
'Neath little Penydarren's load,

A huffing steam loco
Would change the world this day,
It broke each bit of track
But persevered,
Made it all the way,

(Do you hear in the wind
Echoes of the past?
Hammer on anvil
Memories that last?)

That's what Merthyr does
It perseveres,

Pit-scarred hills spring new foliage
It grows more abundant
Every year,

"More than a land of hopes and dreams,
Merthyr is the people... Merthyr is a team!"

And the Martyrs stand tall
Steeled with determination to score,
An Iron will,
Showcasing heart and skill
Spurred on by the crowd's roar,

Just like Trevithick's loco
The mighty Martyrs,
Strong and resilient
Always ready for more...

(Puffing along it
Breaks the tracks, strange contraption
Breaking new ground too)

"More than a land of hopes and dreams,
Merthyr is the people... Merthyr is a team!"

Rhiannon Owens
(Inspired by Merthyr FC and Merthyr Tydfil – the town that has become my
home)

This poem made it into the match program...

'The Martyrs' Issue No. 6 of the 22/23 season
Merthyr Town v Winchester City (27/09/22)

VAYNOR:

Courtesy of Nadine Williams taken June 2022

Vaynor is derived from the Welsh word 'Van' meaning high or lofty. Other spellings such as Faenor or Vainor are possibly of early Irish origin.
The parish of Vaynor contains two river valleys, the Taff Fechan and the Taff Fawr.

,

The Golden One

A mirror of blue
And glowing gold,
From over the hill
Dawn's coming... behold,

Reflection on water
Blue sky and the sun,
A burning heat haze welcomes...
The Golden One.

Ashley O'Keefe
(Inspired by a beautiful Nadine Williams photograph)

Pontsticill Reservoir
Courtesy of Nadine Williams taken June 2022

A Place of Dreams

Mountainous, heavy rainfall
Bridges and streams,
The Parish of Vaynor
A place of dreams,

At dawn's coming, the sun rises
On the horizon to the east,
Bringing gold to this setting
On its beauty, we all feast,

Stories told of its history
Through the passage of time,
Artists with brush strokes
And poets in rhyme,

Romans and Castles
Iron masters, rising men,
A composer, an inventor
Authors and writers with pen,

A Martyr gave her name
To a flourishing town,
On the outskirts stands Vaynor
Wearing her beautiful crown,

Cefn to Trefechan
Ponsticill to Pontsarn,
Vaynor's door is always open
Its people... not born in a barn.

Ashley O'Keefe
(The meaning of 'born in a barn' - To be considered ill-mannered for leaving
an exterior door open)

The Old Parish of Vaynor

Fields and hedges
Houses and farms,
Rivers and streams
Chapels and barns,

A church in a parish
An idyllic place,
Rural and peaceful
Time passing gently with grace...

Fields and hedges
Houses and farms,
Rivers and streams
Chapels and barns,

Two old local customs
On a Wedding Day,
Believing evil spirits
Would be kept away,

Farmers firing shotguns
Into the air,
As the Wedding progresses
Without a care,

Fields and hedges
Houses and farms,
Rivers and streams
Chapels and barns,

Lighting a bonfire
In the churchyard,
Fed by each well-wisher

With a branch to discard,

Fields and hedges
Houses and farms,
Rivers and streams
Chapels and barns.

Ashley O'Keefe
(Inspired by Elwyn Bowen's book, VAYNOR)

A Wedding at St Gwynnos Church Vaynor c1875
Illustration by Dewi Bowen
Courtesy of Liz Bowen

A Traveller Through Faenor (Vaynor) in the 1700s

(This is what a traveller might have seen walking through Vaynor)

High mountain peaks
Thickly strewed with stone,
Bedecked with vegetation
Flowers and ivy grown,

Valleys of grass
Valleys of corn,
Sheep and cattle
Graze at dawn,

Along the river valley
Saluted by rocky precipice,
Ridges of limestone
In abundance, perilous,

Hermits...
In this solitary place,
Dwell half hidden
Tremendous oaks hide their face,

A rural church
Neglected and in decay,
Dark clouds are brewing
I'll be on my way,

A pitiless storm
Drives me to seek,
The Halfway Inn shelter
And a language I can't speak.

Ashley O'Keefe
(Inspired by Elwyn Bowen's book, VAYNOR)

Old Vaynor Church
Illustration by Dewi Bowen
Courtesy of Liz Bowen

The original Vaynor church was built around 800AD and was burnt down during the Battle of Maes-y-Faenor which took place in 1291. The Old Vaynor church built to replace this became dilapidated by 1867 and the Crawshays had a new church built in 1870 on a different site. The church is dedicated to St Gwynno.

Courting In Bed

Secretive and surreptitious
'Courting in bed',
An old-fashioned custom
Sometimes called 'Bundling' instead,

The man throws a pebble
At the window above,
The girl's face appears
Brightly beaming in love,

Climbing a ladder
He'd enter her boudoir,
And leave the same way
Before the rise of dawn's star,

Yet, an unwanted suitor
Could find himself drenched,
With a bucket of swill
Having to leave with the stench.

Ashley O'Keefe
(Inspired by Elwyn Bowen's book, VAYNOR)

The Church of Vaynor

An unassuming portal
A rope dangling from above,
From a stairless tower,
Two tiny bells to sing their love,

Removing my hat, treading carefully
I wander down the aisle,
As the hot sun pours its brilliant rays
Through the stained-glass windows from the sky,

Settling in mellow radiance
Along those empty pews,
And across the deserted altar
Where it lingers in shaded hues.

Ashley O'Keefe
(Inspired by Elwyn Bowen's book, VAYNOR)

St Gwynnos, Vaynor Church,
Courtesy of Molly O'Keefe taken April 2022

Leaves Have Fallen

Air so fresh
Upon the breeze,
In cloud, partly covered
The moon shines through trees,

Aching limbs groan
Against wind and wing,
To the sound of psithurism
Those ancient spirits sing,

Songs and stories
Old and wise,
Full of wisdom
They mesmerise,

Gnarled trees cry
Their leaves have fallen,
Onto shadowy graves
'Tis the time of Autumn,

Moss-laden headstones
In silence, they lean,
Ailing and tilting
Better days they've seen,

A lonely church
Now barely stands,
Crumbling to ruin
Maintenance it demands,

The weathering of centuries
Echoes the pain,
The grief, the loss

The love, the rain.

Ashley O'Keefe
(Inspired by the Old Vaynor Church)

Old Vaynor Church,
Courtesy of Molly O'Keefe taken April 2022

The Tower Stands Alone

Down from the castle
The soldiers came...

    First built of wood
    A timber frame...

Set ablaze overnight...

    Rebuilt of stone...

Before the battle of Maes-y-Faenor...

    Now the tower stands alone.

Ashley O'Keefe

Old Vaynor Church
Watercolour by local artist Ken Morgan

Rural Charm

From the castellated ruins
A panorama of rural charm,
White-washed were the farms
The scenery so calm,

Green sward and hedges
Running wild all around,
In the cloistral silence
Old Vaynor Church could be found,

Lulled into sleep
By the murmuring brook,
All sound was hushed
Until upward I looked,

The plaintive cry
Of the curlew up high,
Lit by the morning sun
In a joyous dawning sky.

Ashley O'Keefe

Resting in Ruins

Standing high on a hill
Of natural limestone,
Upon an Iron Age hillfort
A castle was grown,

Looking over a river
The Taf Fechan; the 'Great Stream',
So that's how they named it
'Mawr Glais' (Morlais) Castle, with esteem,

A defendable escarpment
Built by Gilbert de Clare,
Overlooking Brecknockshire
To extend control from his lair,

Now resting in ruins
Debris from towers with a crypt,
Dismantled with time
Its stones have been stripped,

But still a great view
In those distant skylines,
And as the sun rises
On its battlements, it shines.

Ashley O'Keefe
(Inspired by the ruins of Morlais Castle above Merthyr Tydfil)

Morlais Castle
Courtesy of Molly O'Keefe taken April 2022

Built around 1270 by Gilbert de Clare, the Earl of Gloucester and Lord of Glamorgan, on land claimed by Humphrey de Bohun, where a dispute culminated in the Battle of Maesvaynor or Maes y Faenor, in 1291.
It was briefly held by Welsh rebels three years later, during the Welsh Rebellion. Edward I won the war against the rebels and destroyed parts of the castle to prevent it from ever being used as a stronghold again.

Field of Slaughter (Cae Burdydd)

Protracted disputes
Norman warlords,
Greedy for land
Fighting over their wards,

Humphrey de Bohun
Gilbert de Clare,
From the walls of his castle
Over Humphrey's land, Gilbert's stare,

Across the river
The boundary between,
Gilbert would push
But Humphrey's foreseen,

Vaynor Church, set on fire
De Clare's men routed,
Retreating to Morlais
De Clare not reputed,

In a field below the Castle
Two armies stood,
Not knights on their steeds
More like farmers for the good,

VIOLENCE... CARNAGE...
BLOOD flowed like streams,
One of many clashes
THIS ONE... of extremes.

Ashley O'Keefe
(Inspired by the burial mound at Pontsarn near the Spanish House)

Illustration by Dewi Bowen
Courtesy of Liz Bowen

The old burial mound is called 'Cae Burdydd' and translates as 'Field of Slaughter'. It was given the name in the 1830s after the 1820s excavation which found human remains. It is assumed, where the dead from the Battle of Maes-y-Faenor were buried. It is likely they were buried elsewhere but the remains accidently dug up and reburied/interred in the motte.

Bones Sleep

Soil unearthed
By heavy rain,
The crown of a skull
Displaying the pain,

Echoes of happenings
In a distant past,
When and how
Memories that last,

Ripping, popping
Ligaments tear,
Breaking like sticks
Bones burst in the air,

Bones of hands
Bones of feet,
Bones half chewed
Bones half buried, now sleep.

Ashley O'Keefe

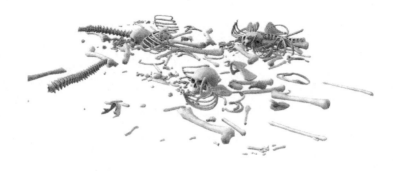

To Dust

A shard so sharp
A heart in two,
Sliced with pain
A sword run through,

A lip that quivers
Eyes filled with mist,
Overflowing with tears
That will soon exist,

Like an old stone ruin
That's met its end,
Fallen, broken
No way to mend,

Time has passed
It won't stand still,
Skin shed by souls
To dust the hill.

Ashley O'Keefe

The Spanish House

The Old Spanish House
Stands empty, looks sad,
Neglected, run-down
With a history, said my Dad,

Let me take you back
To when it was Vaynor Cottage,
In the place called Pontsarn
And a story of passage…

He leaves his house
Just after dawn
On each and every morn,
Walks down to the train station
With a sullen face
His heart; simply torn...

He leaves the train station
Just after dusk
Each and every evening,
Walks back to his door
The house dark; unlit
Inside it should be beaming,

This is his life
These are his days
To work, then home
Never contemplating holidays,
To far off lands
Maybe Rome
To maybe meet someone
Then build a home...

A few years pass
There's not much change
Bed to work, a simple sigh,
But as the sun sets in a red sky
There's a look, a smile,
A glint in his eye...

On holiday in Rome
He met her by chance,
A beautiful Contessa
Through narrow streets, they would dance,

They dined, they laughed
They fell in love,
They spent nights together
Sent their messages by dove,

He came back home
Soon she would follow,
In love and in marriage
Maybe tomorrow,

He built her a house
Extending his home,
Into a Spanish-Italian villa
To bring her from Rome,

Adding two Venetian towers
With stone mullioned window,
Columns and archways
Veranda with balustrades for show,

He waited and waited
But she never came,
Just a dream of love

Unfulfilled again,

Now he leaves his house
Just after dawn
On each and every morn,
Walks down to the train station
With a sullen face
His heart; simply torn...

He leaves the train station
Just after dusk
Each and every evening,
Walks back to his door
The house dark; unlit
Where inside it should be beaming.

Ashley O'Keefe

The Spanish House (Hy Brasail)
Courtesy of Molly O'Keefe taken April 2022

Into the Mist

Disappearing into the mist
Marching sandaled feet,
Echoing into the distance
Through bare branches comes the sleet,

The Romans left their mark
Upon this historic land,
Across the old Sarn Helen road
Where Celts fought and made their stand,

Echoing in the distance
Marching sandaled feet,
Lost in the mists of time
Through bare branches comes the sleet.

Ashley O'Keefe

The Aberglais

The coming of the railway
To this charming countryside,
The Old Parish of Vaynor
Over the Bridge of the Long Road, we would ride,

The original 18th century bridge
Long since replaced by stone,
The Blue Pool and its waterfall
Such natural beauty, this is home,

At the Aberglais, the small Glais brook
Nears its junction at the river,
Hence the name of this Inn
Where home-made hospitality, they deliver.

Ashley O'Keefe
(The meaning of Pontsarn is probably 'The Bridge of the Long Road'
from the ancient times of the Romans)

The Aberglais Hill *(from the Blue Pool)*
Watercolour by local artist Ken Morgan

The Aberglais
Courtesy of Melanie Evans-Jenkins

The Old Swing

Creaking... Swaying...
In the breeze,
By the reservoir
Beneath the trees,

Abandoned... Forgotten...
Memories of laughter and joy,
Smiling faces
Girls and boys,

Dreams of summer
Childhood fun,
Oh, to return
Wondrous days in the sun,

Where are they gone?
Where have they been?
Never to return
To this picture-perfect scene.

Ashley O'Keefe
(Inspired by a Nadine Williams photograph)

Pontsticill Reservoir
Courtesy of Nadine Williams taken 2021

Fields of Green

The natural beauty of a landscape
Untouched serenity in fields of green,
A masterpiece recreated on canvas
For over two hundred years that's the way that it's been,

Below a proud hill covered in history
Of castle ruins some centuries old,
Where a Sanitorium hospital was opened
For the sunny views and its fresh air like gold,

In this old parish of Vaynor
Popular for its days out in the countryside,
A WATER TREATMENT LOCATION TO BE SITED?
Then, Pontsarn's beauty in our children's future...

Will have died.

Ashley O'Keefe
(Written during the Save Pontsarn Campaign 2022)

The Sanitorium Hill (Pontsarn Hill)
Courtesy of Alan George's Old Merthyr Tydfil
http://www.alangeorge.co.uk

84

A Thousand Faces

A boulder with a thousand faces
Shows the blood, sweat and tears,
From the time of a quiet farming valley
To an industrial town's poverty and fears,
From Merthyr town's uprising
To the gallows at Cardiff gaol,
Where a young scapegoat was left to hang
And a thousand faces left to bawl.

Ashley O'Keefe
(Inspired by a Gerald Jones photograph)

Graig-y-Twynau
Courtesy of Gerald Jones taken June 2022

Twynau-Gwynion limestone Quarries above Pant was developed by the Dowlais Iron Company in the 19th century.

Two Rivers Rising

In the wide valley
Beneath the two highest peaks,
Two rivers rising
The south they seek,

Impounded by dams
Forming successive reservoirs,
Through conifer trees
They sneak under the stars,

The Taff Fechan and Taff Fawr
At a confluence they meet,
To become that one river
Below Cefn Coed they greet,

Once heavily polluted
By an industrial past,
Now one of the best waters
Salmon and trout have amassed,

Through Pontypridd and Cardiff
And to Cardiff Bay,
The River Taff flows gently
Into the Severn Estuary clay.

Ashley O'Keefe
(The two highest peaks being Pen-y-Fan and Corn Du)

Pontsticill Reservoir with Corn Du and Pen-y-fan
Watercolour by local artist Ken Morgan

Voices

Leaves... damp, decaying
Hide in ghostly mist,
A smoke covered river
Trees that creak and twist,

A dank musky odour
The sound of emptiness,
Echoes in the distance
From voices long at rest.

Ashley O'Keefe

It Dreams

A dense moss covering
On the trunk of a tree,
Above a blue pool
Grey squirrels scurrying free,

Deciduous oaks
Scattered amongst autumn leaves,
Beneath their spreading boughs
The Taff Fechan weaves,

Through gorge and waterfall
Pool and streams,
Its flowing river
Of the sea, it dreams.

Ashley O'Keefe

Taf Fechan River (Blue Pool)
Courtesy of Molly O'Keefe taken April 2022

The Blue Pool

At Pontsarn, there's a bridge
Spanning a narrow river,
Rushing, cascading,
Through a gorge, feel the quiver,

A beautiful spot
Picturesque, unseen,
Where a waterfall tumbles
Into a blue pool extreme.

Ashley O'Keefe

Blue Pool (Pontsarn)
Courtesy of Molly O'Keefe taken April 2022

Worn is the Rock

Different shapes
Different forms,
Worn is the rock
Over a thousand storms,

A beautiful place
Tranquil and calm,
The susurration of the river
Like a soothing balm,

Verdant trees
The whispering breeze,
Soon will come...
Winter's freeze.

Ashley O'Keefe
(Inspired by Ken Morgan and his beautiful painting of the Taf Fechan gorge below The Blue Pool)

Taf Fechan Gorge
Watercolour by local artist Ken Morgan

Winter's Dream

The river's path meanders
Through overhanging trees,
From the bridge, I look down
Below the waters freeze,

Frost covered branches
An ice-covered stream,
A river coldly flowing
Through a Winter's dream.

Ashley O'Keefe

View of the Taf Fawr River from the Cefn Cemetery bridge
Photograph by Ashley O'Keefe taken 2021

In the Moment

Walking in the moment
Birds sweetly sing,
Their chorus, their melodies
In the tree and on the wing,

The sun shining brightly
Embrace its warming glow,
Below the bridge, the river
Its musty, earthy flow.

Ashley O'Keefe

Pwll Taf, Cefn Coed
Photograph by Ashley O'Keefe taken 2022

Two Rivers Meet

Cefn Coed-y-cymmer
Where two rivers meet,
At the back of the woods
Once a dormitory village with a street,

Dependant on the ironworks
Dependant on coal,
Dependant on the quarries
And the rivers that flow,

The Taf Fechan from the east
The Taf Fawr from the west,
Meets at its confluence
Into the River Taff, unsupressed,

Both rivers rising
Beneath Pen-y-Fan and Corn Du,
From east and from west
Flowing south, to the sea.

Ashley O'Keefe

**The Taf Fawr and Taf Fechan Rivers
meeting below Cefn Coed.**
Photographer Unknown

Cefn Coed-y-cymmer:

The Origin of Cefn Coed-y-cymmer

A large tract of woodland
Covering Cilsanws Mountain slope,
Wildlife teemed in deep recesses
The poachers illicit craft gives life hope,

But the woods were denuded
Stripped of its trees,
Providing fuel to smelt iron
Where Cefn Coed would appease,

A small, picturesque village
Where two rivers meet,
The houses kept rising
And in between, a high street.

Ashley O'Keefe
(Inspired by Elwyn Bowen's book, VAYNOR)

Cefn Coed from Cilsanws in the late 1800's.
Courtesy of Alan George's Old Merthyr Tydfil
http://www.alangeorge.co.uk

The Silent Finger

The silent finger pointing...
Calls the people to worship and pray,
A calling from a higher place
A sanctuary where they can stay,
The spire above the tower
Bells ringing out spreading the faith,
The silent finger pointing...
To the heavens giving the strength of the liath.

Ashley O'Keefe
(Inspired by Dewi Bowen and his illustration of St. John's Church,
Cefn Coed-y-cymmer)

NB: Liath meaning grey, as in the colour of the slate and stone of the church

St JOHN'S CHURCH – CEFN COED – Y- CYMMER
WAS CONSECRATED AND OPENED ON APRIL 20th 1874

Sunshine On the Hill

My Great Mam-gu owned Brynheulog
A house made from river stone,
She carried from the Taf Fechan
Jane Roderick built her home,

A small holding on the mountainside
Along the old Black Patch,
With her family, pigs and chickens
But to eat, they had to catch,

With greenhouses and vegetable gardens
Complete self-sufficiency,
In the cellar all the aunties
Made brawn and faggotts for tea,

Life was so much simpler then
Just a beautiful time to be,
Living off the land
Within your family's company,

The seasons changed, years moved on
And time just won't stand still,
Dark days approached, shadows were cast
They hung over the hill,

As the bird of morning's dawn awoke
As that bird began to crow,
It was one of the saddest days
The family sold up and had to go,

Yes, the family came to sell it
Still such a bitter pill,
The day they came to leave

Their Sunshine on the Hill.

Ashley O'Keefe
(Dedicated to my Great Mam-gu, Jane Roderick Davies who built Brynheulog on Cilsanws Mountain and Rodericks Row in Pontycapel Road, Cefn Coed in the early 1900s. Brynheulog means Sunny Hill or Sunshine on the Hill)

Jane Roderick Davies
Courtesy of Joan Johnson

Stand and Yearn

The cenotaph in Cefn Coed
Commemorates the loss,
Of all its Vaynor residents
Who lay in fields with a cross,

In two world wars they fought
Sadly never to return,
To their home and their loved ones
With their family we stand and yearn,

In honour of their memory
In honour of the brave,
Who gave their lives for freedom
For our lives they died to save.

Ashley O'Keefe
(Dedicated to the brave men of the Parish of Vaynor)

Cefn Coed Cenotaph
Courtesy of Melanie Evans-Jenkins

Unveiled in 1924, the memorial commemorates the residents of the parish of Cefn Coed-y-cymmer who were killed or missing in the First and Second World Wars.

The Hunt

Here comes the hunt
On this autumnal morning,
The haze from the east
The hounds exploring,

In search of a fox
Who hasn't slept in his bed,
He's been out all night
Now so tired, but fed,

Cunning and crafty
With panting breath,
He's been running away
From the hounds seeking death,

Crossing the river
He hides deep in a hole,
For the hounds to move on
They'll not feed on his soul.

Ashley O'Keefe
(Inspired by an old John Yates photograph under Cefn Viaduct)

At Least

The old school echoes silence
At least it does today,
Those walls will soon come crashing down
Another blue sky turning grey,

This place once taught me who I am
It taught my mother and daughters too,
Times they change, they move along
It's sad, but this is true,

Corridors and classrooms
More echoes from the past,
Now stand stale and empty
But friend's and teacher's memories last,

Many are no longer with us
At least they're not today,
But thoughts of them pass through my mind
And will again someday.

Ashley O'Keefe
(Dedicated to both my local schools in Cefn Coed, Ysgol-y-Graig and
Vaynor & Penderyn)

The words of this poem were sent to the talented Declan O'Connell who
added his magic and came up with a song called 'The Old School'.

Walk with a Smile

Green in the sunlight
Of tree and birdsong,
Like a quilt in the springtime
Where blue skies follow dawn,
Rolling to the horizon
Pathways branch through this land,
I walk with a smile
Choices and discoveries in my hand.

Ashley O'Keefe

Taff Trail (Pontsarn)
Photograph by Ashley O'Keefe taken 2022

To Cefn

A pathway leads to Cefn
Along the historic Taff Trail,
Where once the steam trains rode
Upon Crawshay's sleepered rail,

Now a misty Sunday morning
Broken by the sun,
St John's Church in the distance
Where many a hymn's been sung.

Ashley O'Keefe
(Inspired by a Hannah Elizabeth Davies photograph)

Taff Trail (Cefn Coed)
Courtesy of Hannah Elizabeth Davies taken 2021

Covering of Snow

Branches bow and bend
Under a covering of snow,
Beneath, a pathway, powdered white
Footprints come and go,

Walking up 'The Old Line'
Along the new 'Taff Trail',
Kicking up our heels
Where once lay sleeper and rail,

A place of childhood memories
A place of childhood friends,
A place where we made friendships
The kind that never ends.

Ashley O'Keefe
(Inspired by a Deborah Evans photograph)

Taff Trail (Trefechan)
Courtesy of Deborah Evans taken in 2017

Vaynor's Green Quilt

Corn gives way to concrete
Houses rise, another one's built,
Amidst delightful surroundings
Cemented exteriors cover Vaynor's green quilt,

Pastures give way to pylons
In such a pretty place,
An estate grows called Trefechan
For families to embrace.

Ashley O'Keefe

Trefechan – 1957
Courtesy of the Alan George Old Merthyr Tydfil Site
Photograph by Terrance Soames, Cardiff

Poking the Fire

Down from the mountain
In the brilliant summer heat,
You can smell their tiny droppings
On the soles of your feet,
Looking into people's gardens
You can see what came before,
There's torn up lettuce and cabbages
Vegetables chewed about the floor,
At night-time in your bed
You hear them rummage in your bin,
A saucepan of water through the window
Will stop their bloody din,
Then early in the morning
As you try to poke the fire,
Behind you there's a sheep
Standing there like he's the squire.

Ashley O'Keefe
Inspired by the Trefechan Sheep Nuisance film of 1966
https://www.youtube.com/watch?v=1GXYqaoYyGs

CYFARTHFA:

CYFARTHFA CASTLE
Courtesy of Molly O'Keefe taken April 2022

Once home to the Crawshay family, this castellated mansion commanded a view of the valley and of the ironworks of which they were the ironmasters.

Built in 1825 for William Crawshay II using locally quarried stone, it was sold to the council in 1908 and later used as a museum and school.

Stirring Up Memories

An oil-slicked canvas
The end of a summer's day,
Coloured layers floating
In a blue and silver grey,

A distant past echoes
Of furnaces and smoke,
Stirring up memories
Fires no longer stoke,

Reflections of a time
Whispers across the lake,
Calling for 'Bread and cheese'
And a martyr, we'll never forsake.

Ashley O'Keefe
(Inspired by a Melanie Evans-Jenkins photograph)

Cyfarthfa Park Lake at Sunset
Courtesy of Melanie Evans-Jenkins

The Place of Barking Hounds

A castellated mansion
Commanding a great scene,
Of valley and of ironworks
Crawshay's rags and riches scheme,

Cyfarthfa, 'the place of barking'
Where hunting dogs were heard,
The home of ironmasters
In a place; where molten metal stirred,

Every evening from its windows
A glow, a wondrous sight,
Across the way, those ironworks
Lit up the darkest night,

The pounding and the clanking
The flame of furnace roar,
The billowing smoke from chimney stacks
The masters wanting more.

Ashley O'Keefe
(Cyfarthfa loosely translates from Welsh as 'the place of barking' as hunting dogs were regularly heard in this area of the town).

Pont y Cafnau Bridge (Bridge of Troughs)
Illustration by Dewi Bowen
Courtesy of Liz Bowen

Built by Watkin George in 1793 to carry both a tramway for limestone and an aqueduct to carry water to the Cyfarthfa Ironworks.

4 Chapel Row

Northwest of the town
West of the River Taff,
Built in the eighteen twenties
For Crawshay's humble staff,

Built from locally sourced materials
On the outskirts of the town,
Merthyr's natural resources
Limestone, sandstone, trees cut down,

A typical two-storey house
In a terraced row,
A slate-roof; continuous
Small pane windows; candle glow,

A cottage for the ironworkers
The birthplace of a man,
A famous Welsh composer
Of Myfanwy, Welshmen sang.

Ashley O'Keefe
(Inspired by Joseph Parry's Cottage)

Joseph Parry's Cottage
Courtesy of Molly O'Keefe taken April 2022

Far Beyond... and Further

In the hearts of this town's people
He holds a special place,
His music sung by congregations and choirs
Throughout the land of Wales,
And far beyond... and further
No Welsh musician has received such acclaim,
Bringing his music to life with fervour
Joseph Parry, the composer's name.

Ashley O'Keefe

The Old Pandy Clock

At first a fine stone farmhouse
Then a tower with a mechanical clock,
The sound could be heard half a mile away
With its chimes and its tic toc,

With clock faces on three sides
And a blank face that they say,
Was because the builders didn't want to give
Crawshay the time of day.

Ashley O'Keefe

The Pandy Farm
Watercolour by local artist Ken Morgan

COAL:

CASTLE PIT, TROED-Y-RHIW
Illustration by Dewi Bowen
Courtesy of Liz Bowen

This pit was sunk in 1866 by the Crawshay Brothers of the Cyfarthfa Iron Company.

Coal Dust in Our Dreams

Working the coal
Fashioning the seams,
Nothing but black
And coal dust in our dreams,

Out of the darkness
We emerge in dim light,
Then go home to bed
To rest for the night,

We awake the next morning
Before the singing lark,
Once more to descend
Deep, down into the dark.

Back into the blackness
Fashioning the seams,
Then back home to bed
Coal dust in our dreams.

Ashley O'Keefe

Illustration by Dewi Bowen
Courtesy of Liz Bowen

Tunnels

An abandoned mine
A history of men,
Echoes of footsteps
A damp stagnant den,

Into the blackness
The arteries of the earth,
Infinite tunnels
No end, no more worth,

Leading to nowhere
Into dark, into cold,
Time to go back
Into the rays of gold.

Ashley O'Keefe

The Mountain Moves

Rain... the rain...
A heavy downpour,
Days… for days
Saturating the floor,

The mountain moves
The mountain slips,
The slurry slides
The mountain tips,

Children, the children
Mothers call from their bed,
Darkness, the darkness
Fills the morning with dread,

The mountain moves
The mountain slips,
The slurry slides
The mountain tips,

Rumble, the rumble
From the classroom, they peer,
Teachers, the children
To the window, in fear,

The mountain moves
The mountain slips,
The slurry slides
The mountain tips,

Rain, the rain
Spoil turns to slurry,
Shadow, the shadow

Down the mountain, hurry,

The mountain moves
The mountain slips,
The slurry slides
The mountain tips,

Under desk, under table
They all try to hide,
From the roar, the rumble
The thunderous dark tide,

The mountain moves
The mountain slips,
The slurry slides
The mountain tips,

Through windows, through walls
It's total devastation,
Engulfed, entombed
The effect on a nation,

Stillness... the silence
Shadows abound,
No sign of life
No movement, no sound,

Children, the children
The angels call from their bed,
Families, for their families
There're many tears to be shed,

A mountain moved
A mountain slipped,
The slurry slid down

A mountain tipped…

… A mountain slope above a village
Over a natural stream,
A stockpile of spoil
The waste from a colliery coal seam.

Ashley O'Keefe
(In memory of those who lost their lives in the Aberfan Disaster, 21st October 1966)

Aberfan Disaster
Photograph credit to rightful owner

Angel Bells Ring

In a sombre air
A Welsh choir sing,
Is this all in my head?
Angel bells ring,

Homes deserted
An empty street,
Up at the school
The hurrying feet,

Walking up the hill
Tired and weary,
Am I in a dream?
My eyes are bleary,

An eerie silence
The birds stop singing,
Can't even hear
The school bell ringing,

The face of a miner
Exhausted, the devastation,
A mother looks on
Worried, the frustration,

I can't see the children
But I know that they're there,
Beneath the ground
Glaring eyes, the despair,

Vic the Policeman
Carries a child,
Through all the people

From the school now defiled,

Over fifty years on
I stand, I stare,
Children's voices echo
I say a little prayer,

Out of the hillside
In the sight of that dark wave,
Those children lay resting
Buried twice in their grave,

In a sombre air
A Welsh choir sing,
Is this all in my head?
Angel bells ring.

Ashley O'Keefe

Miner at the Aberfan Disaster
Photograph credit to rightful Owner

Vic the Policeman at the Aberfan Disaster
Photograph credit to rightful owner

Aberfan Disaster Memorial
Photograph credit to rightful owner

The Aberfan Disaster

The last day before half term…

The rain had fallen for what seemed like forever…

Just after 9.00am on the 21st October 1966, a colliery spoil tip on a mountain slope above the village of Aberfan near Merthyr Tydfil, slid downhill as a slurry, engulfing Pantglais Junior school, killing 116 children and 28 adults…

The children, aged mostly between seven and ten died in their classrooms, as did their teachers…

MERTHYR BOXING LEGENDS:

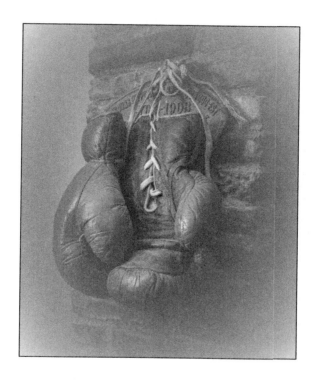

Courtesy of Pixabay

Merthyr has seen many local legends in its time, but some are known world-wide.

Merthyr's Son

Born to Merthyr in Collier's Row
1926 was the start of his show,
Raised on boxing and tales of old
To the fighting game, Eddie's spirit was sold,

A brilliant amateur career
With the ABA Lightweight Title won,
On a professional journey
Arrived a new boxing Son,

A classic style adopted
A beautiful left hand,
With clever footwork
Punches weren't easy to land,

In the coming years
Welterweight Titles he reigned,
The Welsh, British and Empire
Also, the European he claimed,

Listening to the radio
As we ate bara caws,
Hearing Eddie's voice singing
'Bless This House',

As mixed fortunes followed
The time seemed right,
To hang up his gloves
And call it a night,

But this wasn't the end
A new chapter had begun,
Now a coal mine owner

With a business to run,

A world-renowned trainer
And a cutman he'd become,
Who managed Howard Winstone
And Ken Buchanan,

The Mayor of Merthyr
Given the freedom; given the key,
But just five years later
Merthyr's Son's spirit was set free.

Ashley O'Keefe
Dedicated to the memory of Eddie Thomas M.B.E.

Eddie Thomas M.B.E.
Courtesy of Geraint Thomas

When Honourable Men Fought Toe-to-Toe

Merthyr born in nineteen thirty-nine
Of Celtic blood, a Welsh Irish line,
Times were tough, the town was hard
Going through life never off your guard,

When honourable men fought toe-to-toe
And the loser shook hands with his better foe

As a small boy, Howard was often bloody and bruised
By bigger boys who liked to amuse,
"That's it!", his father, Howard Senior did say
And went down on his knees to show Howard the way,

To duck and to weave, to avoid the big blows
No more black eyes or bloody red nose,
The skills that he taught planted the seeds
For the young pretender's forthcoming deeds,

At the age of eleven, Howard wore gloves for the first time
Then proceeded to win like a man in his prime,
From welsh schoolboy, three times champion
He stepped up in class, taking the British title on his second
pass,

When honourable men fought toe-to-toe
And the loser shook hands with his better foe

While working for a living, Howard came off second best
As his fingertips caught in a big power press,
Depressed and handicapped, Howard answered the bell
And came back out fighting, his left jab inflicting hell,

And so, to Cardiff and the Empire games

128

A chance of fortune, an opportunity of fame,
Dreaming of gold and beating the rest
He came back with the gold draped over his chest,

National Service soon came and went
And with an ABA championship under his belt,
The decision was made, it was time to turn Pro
And guided by Eddie, his left jab seemed to flow,

When honourable men fought toe-to-toe
And the loser shook hands with his better foe

Our Welsh Sportsman had won British and European crowns
And with two Lonsdale belts, he was the talk of the town,
The only thing left was a world title shot
Against Ramos or Saldivar, whoever was left in the pot,

The stage was set; the match was on
The two best featherweights, world eyes gazed upon,
Winstone against Saldivar, two contrasting styles
The fans and the crowds came from miles and miles.

Three fights ensued like battles from hell
Titanic struggles from bell to bell,
Bruised and battered, two courageous men
Caused many a writer to pick up their pen,

In the first, Howard's left jab had no chance
Nullified by Saldivar's southpaw stance,
In the second of which he had clearly won
Howard was robbed agreed everyone,

Their final showdown in Mexico
Was a savage encounter trading blow for blow,
Their courage and bravery, their will to survive

Both men giving everything to stay alive,

But in the end, the towel was slung
To the shock and horror of everyone,
Howard was furious, he was still in the race
But a beating he'd taken, to his blood-drenched face,

When honourable men fought toe-to-toe
And the loser shook hands with his better foe

Saldivar retired, his fighting days were done
A vacant world title up for everyone,
And the last chance for Howard as Seki arrived
To bring home that elusive title for which he had strived,

Following a furious toe-to-toe
Seki reeled back from his better foe,
The Referee stepped in and shook his head
And stopped the fight, Seki's eye pumping red.,

A jubilant Howard leapt in the air
All his hard work had finally come to bear,
And as Saldivar presented him with his World title prize
The crowd rose up singing with tears in their eyes,

When honourable men fought toe-to-toe
And the loser shook hands with his better foe

Ashley O'Keefe
(Dedicated to the memory of "The Welsh Wizard" Howard Winstone M.B.E.
a good friend of my father, Brian O'Keefe)

Howard Winstone M.B.E.
Courtesy of Howard Winstone Jr

The Hunger to Win

Strike the match
Ignite the flame,
A boxer was born
To the fighting game,

Fragile in appearance
Painfully thin,
But with phenomenal strength
And the hunger to win,

Hammering pavements
Pounding roads,
Punching bags
And sparring loads,

With a lion's courage
The fight of a bull,
He kept going forward
'Til his scorecard was full,

A setback to progress
Larceny they say,
But revenge was sweet
On Rodriguez that day,

A British Champion outright
With Commonwealth and European Crowns,
Would this proud bantamweight bring
The World Title home to the town?

The World Championship Fight
Abroad in LA,
After twelve gruelling rounds

On the canvas, he lay,

A heart-breaking occurrence
A tragic trick,
His candle went out
But left a smouldering wick…

Ashley O'Keefe
Dedicated to the memory of "The Matchstick Man" Johnny Owen

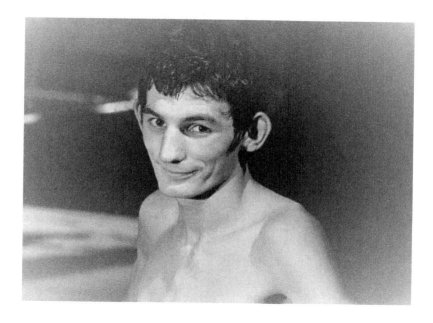

Johnny Owen
Courtesy of Vivian Owen

MERTHYR CHARACTERS:

THE 'LITTLE COLLIER'
Illustration by Dewi Bowen
Courtesy of Liz Bowen

The late Mr Bert Minard of Abercanaid. Winner at the Merthyr Tydfil Carnival 1925.

Teacher Bessie

Bright blue mascara
A touch of rouge,
On delicate cheeks
False eyelashes to choose,

Greased black shining hair
A rounded face,
Soft vermilion lips
A female's grace,

Working for the council
Working on the bins,
Nails varnished; unchipped
Fingers covered in rings,

Unfamiliar at the time
A sight to see,
A transvestite dustman
Who was built like a tree,

His voice; querulous, vibrato
Like Lady Bracknell,
In the Importance of Being Earnest
The way Dame Edith Evans would sell,

Your gaze; drawn toward him
Impossible to ignore,
His eyes would slowly turn away
Contemptuous to deplore,

A strong man, quick-tempered
He could look after himself,
He'd worked as a blacksmith

In the Ivor Works then freed herself,

Away from his day job
At the Merthyr Workmen's Clubs,
He became 'Teacher Bessie'
Dressed in drag in her full scrubs,

Raucous humour he tolerated
Only while he performed,
Offstage no one dared
Such liberties were scorned,

It's a measure of humanity
In our macho Merthyr Town,
To be accepted with amused tolerance
Not persecution or put down.

Ashley O'Keefe
(A Tribute to Willie Pugh known as 'Teacher Bessie')
Thank you to Mr Mario Basini for supplying the information.
RIP Mario Basini.

Photo by Cei Robins https://www.facebook.com/PhotosbyCei/

Willie Pugh (Teacher Bessie)
Courtesy of Dave Robins
Taken by his brother-in-law, Stephen O'Neil

Echoes of Billy Sticks

With a cap and a coat
And a scarf around his neck,
Walking the town
On his daily trek,

Billy the Echo
Billy the Sticks,
Selling his newspapers
Outside the flicks,

Making no profit
Only on tips,
Depositing his pennies
With a smile on his lips,

A true gentleman
A man of such charm,
His spirit walks the town
Echoes under his arm.

Ashley O'Keefe
(A Tribute to Billy Dowling, known as Billy Sticks)

Billy Dowling (Billy Sticks)
Courtesy of Jamie Mahoney

Mathias the Costermonger

A trilby hat and a coat
With a smile he would greet,
A rosy weathered face
Working boots on his feet,

Like Steptoe and Son
With his horse and cart,
He'd come down our street
Selling fruit and veg for a start,

The children would chase
Jump on the back,
Dangle their legs
From Mathias there's no smack,

And any little present
His horse left behind,
With our buckets and shovels
Our gardens it would find,

Then before we knew it
He didn't come anymore,
Time had moved on
With the arrival of the superstore.

Ashley O'Keefe
©2020
(A tribute to Mathias Thomas of Cefn Coed)

Mathias Thomas, the Costermonger c1976
Photographer Unknown

He Wore the Crown

A legend who'd inspire
A legend throughout the town,
A legend in his village
An art teacher of renown,

From Cefn Coed-y-cymmer
To Merthyr Tydfil Town,
An artist of his lifetime
As a gentleman, he wore the crown,

An historian, a storyteller
Touched the lives of all he'd meet,
Over countless decades, loved
Recalling lost memories in the street,

From Cefn Coed-y-cymmer
To Merthyr Tydfil Town,
A legend in his lifetime
A true gentleman, he wore the crown.

Ashley O'Keefe
(A tribute to Dewi Bowen of Cefn Coed-y-cymmer)

Dewi Bowen
Courtesy of Liz Bowen

The Place We Live

Growing up
The place we live,
It moulds our lives
Its dreams it gives,

Shapes us, binds us
Roots us down,
The people, the place
This wonderful town,

An epitome
Of an ancient past,
Through former times
Its history has last.

Ashley O'Keefe
(Inspired by Elwyn Bowen's book, VAYNOR)

Land of Dreams

Land of our fathers
Land of song,
Land of dreams
Where we belong,

Snow-capped mountains
Rivers and streams,
Hills and valleys
The land of dreams,

Steeped in history
Iron and coal,
Through the ages
Welsh passion and soul,

Gwlad ein Tadau
Gwlad y gân,
Gwlad breuddwydion
Ble rydyn yn perthyn.

Erin & Ashley O'Keefe
(A poetic collaboration with my daughter, Erin)

NB: The final stanza is a Welsh translation of the first stanza.

ACKNOWLEDGEMENTS

I didn't just want a book of poems about my hometown, I wanted to share some of the local talent we've had and still have in Merthyr and ask for their help with creating this book, whether it be through illustrations, paintings, photographs or their wonderful inspiration.

Not in any particular order, I'd like to thank:-

Liz Bowen for allowing me to use her uncle Dewi's amazing illustrations which help bring my poems to life.

The late Mr Dewi Bowen for his amazing art and inspiration.

The late Mr Elwyn Bowen, father of Liz and Brother to Dewi, and my former headmaster at Ysgol-y-Graig Junior School, Cefn Coed. His book VAYNOR inspired so many poems about the parish.

Lynette Rees, author, whose book 'The Workhouse Waif' inspired a whole section of poems about 1800s Merthyr.

G I Lewis, author of 'The Ghosts of China' whose inspiration added to the 1800s section.

Ken Morgan, local watercolour artist, whose work complemented my poems beautifully.

My daughter Molly O'Keefe for her beautiful photography and the precious time we spent travelling around the area to get the photographs.

My daughter Erin for our beautiful poetic collaboration.

Local friends and neighbours whose photographs of the surrounding scenery always inspire me to write:-

Nadine Williams
Melanie Evans-Jenkins
Hannah Elizabeth Davies
Deborah Evans
Gerald Jones

Those of you who gave permission to use their photos:-

Joan Johnson
Geraint Thomas
Howard Winstone Jr
Vivian Owen
Dave Robins & Stephen O'Neil
James Mahoney

Christopher Parry and Cyfarthfa Castle Museum and Art Gallery for kindly letting me use one of their images.

Alison Davies for her amazing knowledge of Merthyr's past.

Last but not least, my special thanks to my super talented writing partner, Rhiannon Owens for her editing, photograph and poetic contribution.

My appreciation goes out to you all.

Also images courtesy of
Pixabay.com, Florida Center for Instructional Technology
& Rob Amos

DEDICATIONS

I'd like to dedicate this book to two brothers who have brought so much interest, knowledge, art and heritage to our town:-

The late Elwyn and Dewi Bowen

Dr Elwyn Bowen MBE

A true scholar and family man, Mr Bowen was my headmaster in Ysgol-y-Graig Junior School and would always share old stories with his pupils about Vaynor. If only I could recall them, 50 years on. Mr Bowen did, however, publish a book about his beloved Vaynor many years later which was illustrated by his brother.

I remember Mr Bowen always telling us as pupils to 'tip our caps' or raise our hand to touch the side of our head in salute as a way of greeting or acknowledging someone as we passed them by.

Mr Dewi Bowen

An inspiring and popular art teacher at Cyfarthfa School and wonderful artist in his own right. Mr Dewi Bowen portrayed scenes and characters from the rich and colourful history of Merthyr and Cefn Coed-y-cymmer in his own distinctive style and contributed so much to the heritage of our town.

Like his brother, Mr Dewi Bowen was naturally amusing and loved to share stories and make people laugh.

Two brothers... Two legends...

I'd also like to dedicate this book as always to my family here and passed.

OTHER BOOKS
by Ashley O'Keefe

The Rhianno & Asley Collection Series
by
Rhiannon Gwyneth Owens & Ashley O'Keefe

A Voyage of Poetic Discoveries
Seeking Poetic Lands
Seeing with Poetic Eyes
Searching Across Poetic Sands
In Poetic Dreams

*****

The Rhianno & Asley Special Edition Series
by
Rhiannon Gwyneth Owens & Ashley O'Keefe

Nocturnals
Collaborations

https://www.facebook.com/RhiannoAsleyPoetry/

*****

Life, Love, Loss & After
by
Ashley O'Keefe

*****

Printed in Great Britain
by Amazon

16072052R00098